SAY IT AGAIN!

A say-it-yourself guide
to the most commonly
mispronunciated words

by Leila B. Alson and Douglas Kalajian

Praise for *Say It Again!*

"You have created a very practical and useful book to help those who wish to optimize the delivery and effectiveness of the verbalized message. I found several words in your list that I have been mispronouncing. Imagine that!"

—Robert Scalabrini,
CEO, Allied Construction Products, LLC

"Reading *Say it Again!* was almost like playing a game, seeing how many words I actually pronounce correctly. I would especially recommend it to anyone in college and in the job market. Speaking well is very important in making a good impression during an interview. *Say it Again!* is a good reference to have, it is fun and informative at the same time!"

—Louis F. Rose,
DDS, MD

"Imagine being letter-perfect when you speak, creating a truly impressive first-impression and having fun polishing your speaking skills. *Say it Again!* delivers all this and more..."

—Nick G. Costa
Vice President,
Development & Alumni Relations,
Arcadia University

Say It Again
Publishers, LLC

www.SayItAgain.org

Designed by David Blasco
Original cover illustration by Bill Dobkin

'Your speaking style may be the most important part of your image.'

Leila B. Alson

Speak for success

Which would you rather hear: Fingernails scraping on a chalkboard, or one more person saying "nucular" instead of nuclear?

If you unhesitatingly answered, "No more nukes," this book is for you.

But please, don't get sanctimonious and insist you are never judgmental (or, as the late President Gerald Ford liked to say, judge-a-mental) about such things.

Sure you are. We all are, and that's OK.

Speech is our first and best way of gauging a stranger's knowledge, proficiency and professionalism. People who speak clearly and well have a big advantage over fumblers and mumblers.

You know what you want to say

We're going to assume you're not a fumbler. You know what you want to say and you take advantage of a wide and varied vocabulary to say it with style and without ambiguity.

But are you really saying it right?

Everyone makes mistakes.

Would you be perjuring yourself if you denied ever saying per-jorative instead of pejorative?

Do you have a cultural bias against horticulturists that leads you to say horticultur-al-iss?

If you just can't get your foot out of your mouth, will you consult a po-di-AT-trist or a podiatrist?

Even if you're confident of your pronunciation, consider this: If you do make a mistake, you'll be the last one to know. We don't hear ourselves the way others do. And just as you are far too polite to correct your friends, co-workers or maybe even your spouse, most of them are too polite to correct you.

Luckily for you, we're not so polite.

Here's how it works

The advice in the following pages is straightforward and based on traditional, preferred American English pronunciation — with the emphasis on traditional. The goal of this guide is to help you sound polished, not to provide loopholes if you're rousted by the language police. So don't plead that your dictionary accepts "nucular." We will not be disarmed.

Follow this guide and no educated person will snicker when you speak. The method of correction and instruction is fool-proof. We've even tossed in the occasional uncommon word, just to show that nothing's too difficult for you.

Speech coach Leila B. Alson developed this approach while training some of America's most successful public speakers. You might question how a written guide can teach sounds. It doesn't have to.

This guide uses sounds and words you already know as models.

In the Say It Right column, the color green means Go! It's the correct pronunciation. Wherever possible these words contain a familiar, embedded word or sound. Syllabic stress is marked with the symbol '.

In the column entitled Say It Wrong, the color red means Stop!

Say and listen to the word

To change your pronunciation, it's necessary to recognize and identify the target word by saying it aloud. Listen for the error. Now carefully say and listen to the word listed under Say It Right.

Can you tell the difference? Practice several times out loud, being sure to focus on the green segment. Next, practice saying the word in three different sentences, always listening for the target sound or syllable.

You may be surprised to find that some often-mispronounced words are also short and seemingly simple. Iron, for example. Many people in different parts of the country pronounce it "I run."

How to Say It Right? "I earn."

It doesn't get any harder than that, although there is (as always) one sticky little matter. The symbol ∂. We can't tell you how to pronounce it. Not that there's any secret. The poor symbol is just sensitive. The moment it's pronounced, it disappears. Really. Say it and it's gone.

So, we won't say it. Think of it as a sound waiting to happen. Like the "e" in gopher or tuber or rubber. OK? Then let's get down to biz-n∂ss.

Important note: Say It Right uses only the first choice in our reference dictionaries.

Look for the embedded word

Words are listed at left. In the center they are spelled as if they contain a familiar sound or word you know how to say. In the right column the same embedded word technique is used to show how words are often mispronounced.

Word	Say It Right	Say It Wrong
iron	'I EARN	'I RUN

A dandy lion

The words in this section have sounds that are mispronounced or add sounds that were never meant to be there.

	Say It Right	Say It Wrong
across	∂ 'CROSS	∂ 'CROSS T
airplane	'air 'plane	'air OH 'plane
are	'ARR	'ah RUH
arthritis	arth 'RIGHT is	AUTHOR 'itis

	Say It Right	Say It Wrong
athlete	'ATH lete	'ATHUH lete
cacao	c∂ 'CAO	'CO CO
comfort	'COME fort	'CALM fort
dandelion	'DAND∂ LINE	'DANDY LION
escape	ES 'cape	EKS 'scape
especially	ES 'specially	EKS 'specially
film	'FILM	'fil UHM
mine	'MINE	'MY UHN
oriented	'ORIENT ed	'orient ATE d
salmon	'SAM in	'SAL min
spirit	'SPIR("i" as in sit) it	'SPEAR it

Go for the juggler

And then there are words where a sound or sounds are mistakenly eliminated. Sometimes syllables are collapsed, while others disappear entirely. In certain instances when sounds or syllables are omitted, the word mutates into a different meaning.

	Say It Right	Say It Wrong
already	ALL 'ready	∂ 'ready
accelerate	AK 'celerate	∂ 'SELL erate
actually	'ac CHEW ally	'ac SH∂LLY
actuary	'ac CHEW ary	'ac SHOE ary
antioxidant	AUNTIE 'oxidant	ANNIE 'oxidant
battery	'BATTER ee	'ba TREE
business	'BIZ ness	'Bin ess
clothes	'cloTHe z	'CLOSE

	Say It Right	Say It Wrong
crayon	'CRAY on	'CROWN
deteriorate	de 'tere EE OR ate	de 'tere EE ate
disastrous	di 'zass TR∂SS	di 'zass-TER ∂SS
eleemosynary	EL∂ 'mosynary	ELEEO 'mosynary
facsimile	FAC 'simile	FAS 'simile
facts	'fac TS	'FAX
forward	'FOR WARD	'FOE WOOD
frustrate	'FRUS trate	'FUSS trate
golf	'go L f	'GOF
help	'he L p	'HEP

(In help and golf, feel your tongue touch the ridges behind your front teeth after the vowel sounds. This will help you both feel and hear the "l" sound, then add "p" or "f".)

inaugural	i 'naug YOUR al	i 'naug ∂ ral
jugular	'jug YOU ler	'JUGGLER
lecture	'lec CHER	'lec SHER
mayor	'MAY er	'MARE
mercantile	mercan 'TEAL	mercan 'TILE

	Say It Right	Say It Wrong
next	'nexT	'neCKS
particularly	par 'TICKYOU LER ly	par 'TICKLE y
picture	'PICK cher	'PITCH er
probably	'PRAH bubbly	'PROLLY
question	'qwes CHIN	'qweh SHIN
recognize	'wreck ∂G nize	'wreck UH nize
ruin	'rue IN	'ROON
secretary	'sec R∂ terry	'sec∂ terry
seriatim	ser ee 'ATE ∂m	'ser UH tim
specific	SP∂ 'cific	P∂ 'cific
statutory	'stat CH∂ tory	'STATUE tory
succession	SUCK 'cession	SUH 'cession
terrorism	'TERROR ism	'TERR ism
terrorist	'TERROR ist	'TER-ist
vulnerable	'VUL NER ∂ble	'VUH NUH ble
wholesome	'WHOLE some	'HOE some

Ax, or you won't make the cut

Have you ever reversed two numbers in your checkbook and found that you couldn't reconcile your statement?

The same things happen in words when two syllables are transposed. This occasionally occurs because it's easier for the tongue to work in one way than another.

For example, it's easier for the tongue to move from aks than it is to say ask. Try it and feel the difference.

If you do say aks instead of ask, it's not because you're lazy. It's most likely because everyone around you said it that way when you were growing up. It's what we call neighborhood speech, and it's the sort of quirk nobody thinks twice about until you move to another neighborhood.

Just don't get all snooty if nobody in your neighborhood ever "axed" a question. If you're sure you'd never say ax unless you were discussing a weapon, think about whether you ever saw "a play in two ax."

When you read some of the words in this group, you need only to look at the spelling to determine the order of the sounds. It's easy to find the difference.

	Say It Right	Say It Wrong
acts	'ACTS	'AX (aks)
adjective	'ad JIC tive	'ad JUH tive
annualize	'ANNUAL ize	'ANNA lize
ascorbic	∂S 'corbic	AX (aks) 'corbic
ask	'ASS k	'AX (aks)
iron	'i EARN	'i RUN
jewelry	'JEWEL ry	'JEWLER y
larynx	'la RINKS	'lar NICKS
mascarpone	MASCAR 'ponay	MARSCA 'pone
nuclear	'new KLEE er	'new CUE ler
peremptory	PER 'emptory	PREE 'emptory
prerequisite	PREE 'requisite	PER 'requisite
prerogative	PR∂ 'rogative	PER 'rogative
Realtor	'REAL ter	're LUH ter
remunerate	re 'MEW nerate	re 'NEW merate
remuneration	re 'MEW neration	re 'NEW meration

Pitcher perfect

On occasion one sound, group of sounds or syllable is substituted for another.

	Say It Right	Say It Wrong
anecdote	'ANEC dote	'an TIC dote
both	'bo TH	'bo F

	Say It Right	Say It Wrong
conch chowder	'CONK chowder	'CONCH chowder
erudite	'er YOU dite	'ERRUH dite
etcetera	et 'SET era	EK 'setera
gas	'GAS	'GAZ
height	'high T	'hi TH
intellectual	INT∂ 'lec CHEW al	INN∂ 'lec SHOE al
intervention	'INTER vention	'INNER vention
introducing	'INTR∂ ducing	'INNER ducing
library	'li BRAIRY	'li BERRY
machination	'MACK ination	'MATCH ination
picture	'PICK cher	'PITCH er
scapula	'scap YOU la	'scap UH la
subsidiary	sub 'CITY erry	sub 'SIT ER erry
Valentine	'Valen TINE	'Balen TIME

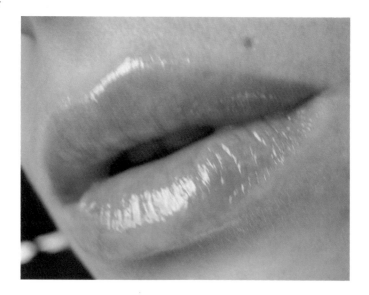

Loose lips cause slips

When certain consonant clusters arise in words, their sounds may become blended into a totally different combination of sounds because the movement of the lips and/or tongue allows another sound to be formed when you don't articulate carefully.

Following is a group of sounds that change character when the lips move forward to pronounce the tr sound. The production of the str moves the lips and tongue to create the shtr.

You might call this the sound of the shtreet. It's most common in cities — you'll even hear it from some well educated, big-city politicians.

The first step to correcting this mispronunciation is to listen for it in others. Once you recognize it, you'll be eager to correct it in your own speech.

To do so, complete the s sound before rounding the lips for tr, i.e., ss...treat, ss...tripe. Once you can keep the s sound clear, you may eliminate the pause.

	Say It Right	Say It Wrong
strategy	'SS TRAT egy	'SHTRAT egy
street	'SS TREAT	'SHTR eet
string	'SS TRING	'SHTR ing
stripe	'SS TRIPE	'SHTR ipe
strong	'SS TRONG	'SHTR ong
structure	'SS TRUCK CHer	'SHTRuck SHer

Now that you've mastered the sound at the beginning of the word, try it in the middle. It's a little harder.

construction	con 'SS TRUCK tion	con SHTRUCK tion
distribution	di SS TRI 'bution	DISH tri 'bution
gastric	'ga SS TRICK	ga SHTRICK
obstruction	ob 'SS TRUCK tion	ob 'SHTRUCK tion
restrict	re 'SS TRICT	re 'SHTRICT
restructure	re 'SS TRUCK CHer	re 'SHTRUCK SHer

Leaning the wrong way

Some words just have the accent on the wrong syllable or stretch the vowel sound in a way that changes the rhythm of the word and draws attention to how you say it rather than what you say. Observe the syllable that is preceded by an accent mark.

	Say It Right	Say It Wrong
affluence	'A flu ens	a 'FLU ens
ambulance	'ambu L∂NS	'ambu LANCE
arbiter	'ar BITTER	'ar BITE R

	Say It Right	Say It Wrong
barbiturate	bar 'BIT urate	barbit 'YOUR ate
comparable	'com PER ∂ble	come 'PAIR ∂ble
derivative	de 'riv ITIVE	derive 'ATE ive
genuine	'genu IN	'genu WINE
impotent	'im P∂T∂NT	im 'POTE ∂nt
inexorably	in 'EX orably	inex 'OR ably
panoply	'pan ∂PLY	'pa NOPOLY
paroxysm	'PAR∂K sysm	par 'ROCK sysm
plethora	'pleth ER∂	pleth 'AURA
police	p∂ 'LEASE	'POE lease
retrospect	'RET rospect	retro 'SPECT
statutory	'stat CH∂ tory	'STATUE tory
theater	'THEE∂ ter	THEE 'ATE er
umbrella	um 'BRELLA	'UMBER ella
urinal	'urine ∂l	urine 'ALL

A matter of law

Following is a group of words and phrases that illustrate the law of physics that states that mat-

ter cannot be created nor destroyed.

We find that a sound that disappears in one location merely relocates, sometimes in the same city and sometimes in another. For example: the r that disappears when the phrase pahk the cah in Boston relocates and may be found in New York, Washington, Baltimore or even in Boston. There's really no telling where the "intrusive r" will turn up, but we know it has traveled as far as Chiner... or even Chiner and Japan.

	Say It Right	Say It Wrong
China	'CHINA	'CHINER
pillow	'pill OH	'pill ER
saw	'SAW	'SAWR
son-in-law	'son-in-'LAW	'son-in-'LAWR
squash	'SKWASH	'skwaRsh
wash	'WASH	'WAR sh
windows	'win DOWS	'wind ERS

Don't resist foreign influence

Does just thinking about EYE'talian food give you heartburn?

Try IT'alian.

Feels better already, doesn't it?

Even if you shift the conversation to this continent, you can't avoid foreign words. Most English words came from some other language, but common words like mayonnaise (French), dollar (Dutch) and data (Latin) have been Americanized. Just like the people who brought them here.

And, just like people, new words arrive daily. Unlike people, you shouldn't feel compelled to welcome them. Sometimes, the best way to avoid sounding foolish by mispronouncing distinctly foreign words is simply to avoid them.

Why ask for au jus when what you crave is

natural gravy? Why order the table d'hote when what you want is a full-course meal? But, if you insist on impressing the waiter, say oh-'zhoo (that "zh" should sound like the "s" in "pleasure") and tah-bl∂ 'dote.

But sometimes there's no good substitution. The trick then is to avoid being tricked and just learn the correct pronunciation.

That way, the impression you make will be a good one. Master all the words in this book and you're sure to make that same good impression on everyone. Your celebration as a master of the language will be a fait accompli.

	Say It Right	Say It Wrong
bona fide	'bona FIDE	'bona FIDEE
chipotle	chi 'POE tlay	chi 'POT tle
croissant	CRWA 'sant	'CROY sant
curriculum vitae	'curric you lum 'VIT∂	'curric you lum 'VITAY
entrepreneur	entre 'PREN ER	entre 'PEN YOUR
prima facie	'prima FAY sh∂	'prima FAH sh∂
voir dire	'VWAR dear	'VOY dear

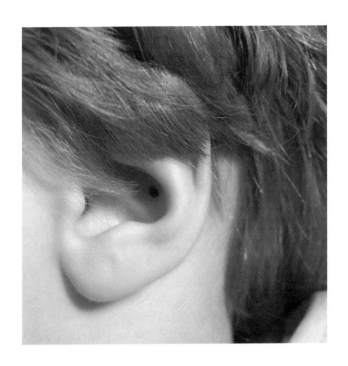

Conclusion:
You heard it wrong!

A challenge:
Mangled words tangle our brains. Sometimes we don't hear a thing that follows because we're so distracted. A really tortured word can get stuck in our heads, like a sour note in a symphony.

Do you have that problem too? If you've read this far, it's a good bet you do. Perhaps we can help. We'd like to get those words out of your head and into our next book. Send us your favorite mispronounced words. If we use them, the three judged most interesting will each receive a free book.

Guide to pronunciation

Here you will find all the words used as examples in each lesson in this book, and more besides.

A

	Say It Right	Say It Wrong
abstract	'abs TRACK t	'ab SHTRACT
accelerate	AK 'celerate	∂ 'SELL erate
across	∂ 'CROSS	∂ 'CROSS T
acts	'ACTS	'AX (aks)
actually	'ac CHEW ally	'ac SH∂LLY
actuary	'ac CHEW ary	'ac SHOE ary
adjective	'ad JIC tive	'ad JUH tive
administration	admini 'STRAY tion	admini 'SHTRAY tion
advantage	ad 'van TIGE	ad 'van IGE
adversary	'ad VERSE ary	'ad VUH sary
advertise	'AD vertise	'A vertise
advocate	'AD v∂cate	'A v∂cate
affluence	'A flu ens	a 'FLU ens
airplane	'air 'plane	'air OH 'plane

	Say It Right	Say It Wrong
almond	'AH m∂nd	'AM m∂nd
already	ALL 'ready	∂ 'ready
ambulance	'ambu L∂NS	'ambu LANCE
anecdote	'ANEC dote	'an TIC dote
annualize	'ANNUAL ize	'ANNA lize
antioxidant	AUNTIE 'oxidant	ANNIE 'oxidant
arbiter	'ar BITTER	'ar BITE R
are	'ARR	'ah RUH
arthritis	arth 'RIGHT iss	AUTHOR 'itis
arthroscopic	ARE thro 'scopic	OR thro 'scopic
ascorbic	∂S 'corbic	AX (aks) 'corbic
ask	'ASS k	'AX (aks)
associates	∂ 'so SEE its	∂ 'so SHE its
athlete	'ATH lete	'ATHUH lete
attentive	∂ 'TENT ive	∂ 'TEN ive

B

barbiturate	bar 'BIT urate	barbit 'YOUR ate

	Say It Right	Say It Wrong
bath	'ba TH	'ba F
bathtub	'BATH 'tub	'BAF 'tub
battery	'BATTER ee	'ba TREE
bonafide	'bona FIDE	'bona FIDEE
both	'bo TH	'bo F

If you say "f" when you want to say "th" put your tongue between your teeth and it becomes easy.

| **business** | 'BIZ ness | 'BIN ess |

C

cacao	c∂ 'CAO	'CO CO
centrifugal	cen 'TRIF igal	centri 'FEW gal
China	'CHINA	'CHINER
chipotle	chi 'POE tlay	chi 'POT tle
clandestine	clan 'des TIN	clan 'des TINE
clothes	'cloTHe z	'CLOSE
collateral	C∂ 'lateral	'COH lateral
comfort	'COME fort	'CALM fort

	Say It Right	Say It Wrong
comparable	'com PER ∂ble	come 'PAIR ∂ble
conch chowder	'CONK chowder	'CONCH chowder
constraints	con 'STRAIN ts	con 'SHTRAIN ts
construction	con 'SS TRUCKtion	con SHTRUCK tion
crayon	'CRAY on	'CROWN
croissant	CRWA 'sant	'CROY sant
curator	'cur ATE or	'CURE ∂tor
curriculum vitae	'curric you lum 'VIT∂	'curric you lum 'VITAY

D

dandelion	'DAND∂ LINE	'DANDY LION
demonstrable	de 'mon STR∂BLE	demon 'STRATE able
dentist	'DENTIST	'DENNIS
derivative	de 'riv ITIVE	derive 'ATE ive
deteriorate	de 'tere EE OR ate	de 'tere EE ate
disastrous	di 'zass TR∂SS	di 'zass-TER ∂SS
distracted	DIS 'tracted	DISH 'tracted

	Say It Right	Say It Wrong
distress	DIS 'tress	DISH 'tress
distribute	DIS 'tribute	DISH 'tribute
distribution	di SS TRI 'bution	DISH tri 'bution
detritus	de 'TRY t∂s	de 'TREAT ∂s

E

eleemosynary	EL∂ 'mosynary	ELEEO 'mosynary
entrepreneur	entre 'PREN ER	entre 'PEN YOUR
escape	ES 'cape	EKS 'scape
erudite	'er YOU dite	'ERRUH dite
especially	ES 'specially	EKS 'specially
etcetera	et 'SET era	EK 'setera
exacerbate	EGZ 'acerbate	EKS 'acerbate
expedite	'ex P∂DITE	ex 'PEEDIATE
extraneous	ek 'STRAIN eous	ek 'SHTRAIN eous

F

facsimile	FAC 'simile	FAS 'simile
facts	'fac TS	'FAX

	Say It Right	Say It Wrong
February	'fe BREW ary	'feb YOU ary
film	'FILM	'fil UHM
foliage	'FOE liage	'FOIL EE age
forward	'FOR WARD	'FOE WOOD
frustrate	'FRUS trate	'FUSS trate

G

gas	'GAS	'GAZ
gastric	'ga SS TRICK	ga SHTRICK
genuine	'genu IN	'genu WINE
golf	'go L f	'GOF
graph	'GRAF	'GRAFT

H

height	'high T	'hi TH
help	'he L p	'HEP

I

idea	i 'DE∂	I 'DEAR

	Say It Right	Say It Wrong
illustration	illu 'STRAY tion	illus 'SHTRAY tion
impotent	'im PəTəNT	im 'POTE ənt
inaugural	i 'naug YOUR al	i 'naug ə ral
industrial	in 'DUST rial	in 'DUSH trial
inexorably	in 'EX orably	inex 'OR ably
instruction	in 'STRUCK tion	in 'SHTRUCK tion
instrument	'in STRUM ent	'in SHTRUM ent
intellectual	INTə 'lec CHEW al	INNə 'lec SHOE al
intercept	'INTER cept	'INNER cept
interchange	'INTER change	'INNER change
intervention	INTER 'vention	INNER 'vention
Intracoastal	'INTRA'coastal	'INTER 'coastal
introduce	'INTRə duce	'INNER duce
introducing	'INTRə ducing	'INNER ducing
iron	'i EARN	'i RUN

J-K

jewelry	'JEWEL ry	'JEWLER y

	Say It Right	Say It Wrong
jugular	'jug YOU ler	'JUGGLER

L

	Say It Right	Say It Wrong
language	'lang WIDGE	'lang WITCH
larynx	'la RINKS	'lar NICKS
lecture	'lec CHER	'lec SHER
library	'li BRAIRY	'li BERRY

M

	Say It Right	Say It Wrong
machination	'MACK ination	'MATCH ination
mammogram	'MAM ∂gram	'MAMMY ∂gram
maraschino	maris 'KEY no	maris 'CHEE no
mascarpone	MASCAR 'ponay	MARSCA 'pone
math	'MATH	'MAF
mayor	'MAY er	'MARE
mercantile	mercan 'TEAL	mercan 'TILE
mine	'MINE	'MY UHN
miniscule	'minis CUE l	'minis CULL
mischievous	'mis CHIV ∂s	mis 'CHEE VEE ∂s

	Say It Right	Say It Wrong
mispronunciation	mis pro'NUNciation	mis pro'NOUNciation
mouth	'mou TH	'mou F

N

next	'nexT	'neCKS
northern	'north EARN	'north ∂RUN
nuclear	'new KLEE er	'new CUE ler

O

obstruct	ob 'STRUCK t	ob 'SHTRUCKt
obfuscate	'ob FUH scate	'ob FEW scate
oriented	'ORIENT ed	'orient ATE d
obstruction	ob 'SS TRUCK tion	ob 'SHTRUCK tion

P

panoply	'pan ∂PLY	'pa NOPOLY
paroxysm	'PAR∂K sysm	par 'ROCK sysm
particularly	par 'TICK YOU LER ly	par 'TICKLE y
peremptory	PER 'emptory	PREE 'emptory
perspiration	PURSE per 'ation	PRESS per 'ation

	Say It Right	Say It Wrong
perspire	PER 'spire	PRE 'spire
picture	'PICK cher	'PITCH er
pillow	'pill OH	'pill ER
plethora	'pleth ER∂	pleth 'AURA
police	p∂ 'LEASE	'POE lease
pomegranate	'pom∂ gran IT	'pom∂ GRANT
premonition	'PREE monition	'PREM onition
prerequisite	PREE 'requisite	PER 'requisite
prerogative	PR∂ 'rogative	PER 'rogative
prescription	PR∂ 'scription	PER 'scription
prima facie	'prima FAY sh∂	'prima FAH sh∂
probably	'PRAH BUBBLY	'PROLLY
prostate	'pro STATE	'pro STRAIGHT
prune	'PRUNE	'pru IN

Q-R

	Say It Right	Say It Wrong
question	'qwes CHIN	'qweh SHIN
Realtor	'REAL ter	're LUH ter

	Say It Right	Say It Wrong
recognize	'rec ∂G nize	'rec UH nize
reconciled	'WRECK ∂n ciled	'REE c∂n ciled
remunerate	re 'MEW nerate	re 'NEW merate
remuneration	re 'MEW neration	re 'NEW meration
residual	re 'ZID ual	re 'SID ual
restrain	re S'TRAIN	re 'SHTRAIN
restrict	re 'SS TRICT	re 'SHTRICT
restructure	re 'SS TRUCK CHer	re 'SHTRUCK SHer
retrospect	'RET rospect	retro 'SPECT
ruin	'rue IN	'ROON

S

salmon	'SAM in	'SAL min
sandwich	'SAND WITCH	'SAM ITCH
saw	'SAW	'SAWR
scapula	'scap YOU la	'scap UH la
secretary	'sec R∂ terry	'sec∂ terry

	Say It Right	Say It Wrong
seriatim	ser ee 'ATE ∂m	'ser UH tim
similar	'SIM iler	'sim YOU ler
simultaneous	SIGH mul 'taneous	SIM mul 'taneous
son-in-law	'son-in-'LAW	'son-in-'LAWR
southern	suth 'EARN	suth 'er RUN
specific	SP∂ 'cific	P∂ 'cific
spirit	'SPIR ("i" as in sit) it	'SPEAR it
splinter	'SPLINT er	'SPLINN er
spoliation	sp OH li 'ation	'SPOIL i'ation
squash	'SKWASH	'skwaRsh
statutory	'stat CH∂ tory	'STATUE tory
strategy	'SS TRAT egy	'SHTRAT egy
strawberry	'STRAW 'berry	'SHTRAw 'berry
streamline	'SSTREAM 'line	'SHTREAM 'line
street	'SS TREAT	'SHTR eet
stretch	'SS TRETCH	'SHTRETCH
string	'SS TRING	'SHTR ing
stripe	'SS TRIPE	'SHTR ipe

	Say It Right	Say It Wrong
strong	'SS TRONG	'SHTR ong
structure	'SS TRUCK CHer	'SHTRuck SHer
struggle	'SS TRUGGLE	'SHTRUGGLE
subsidiary	sub 'CITY erry	sub 'SIT ER erry
succession	SUCK 'cession	SUH 'cession

T

	Say It Right	Say It Wrong
theater	'THEE∂ ter	THEE 'ATE er
teeth	'tee TH	'tee F
tendency	'TENDON cy	'TENNON cy
terrorism	'TERROR ism	'TERR ism
terrorist	'TERROR ist	'TER-ist
toothbrush	'tooTH 'brush	'tooF 'brush
toward	'TORE d	'TO WARD

U-V

	Say It Right	Say It Wrong
umbrella	um 'BRELLA	'UMBER ella
urinal	'urine ∂l	urine 'ALL
Valentine	'Valen TINE	'Balen TIME

	Say It Right	Say It Wrong
vinaigrette	vina 'GRETTE	'VINAGER ette
voir dire	'VWAR dear	'VOY dear
vulnerable	'VUL NER əble	'VUH NUH ble

W-X-Y-Z

	Say It Right	Say It Wrong
wash	'WASH	'WAR sh
wheelbarrow	'wheel 'BARROW	'wheel 'BARREL
wholesale	'WHOLE sale	'HOE sale
wholesome	'WHOLE some	'HOE some
windows	'win DOWS	'wind ERS
winter	'win TER	'WINNER
with	'wi TH	'wi F
withdrawal	with 'DRAW əl	with 'DRAWL
wonderful	'WONDER ful	'WON erful

The authors

Leila B. Alson is a speech coach and certified speech pathologist whose Alson Power Speaking method has helped many prominent business and political leaders become effective public speakers. She has taught at major universities and lectured throughout the United States and interna-  tionally. She is widely quoted in newspapers and magazines and has made numerous television and radio appearances.

She is president of Alson Power Speaking.

 Douglas Kalajian is a retired editor and reporter who has worked at such newspapers as The Miami Herald, The New York Daily News and The Palm Beach Post.

He is also author of the non-fiction book *Snow Blind*.

Please see www.SayItAgain.org for more on Leila Alson's proven method as well as news about upcoming publications.

LaVergne, TN USA
22 August 2009
155625LV00001B

9780615310824